This book belongs to:

_____

What does healthy mean?

We are the most healthy when our bodies and thoughts feel good.

Our bodies can affect the way we think.

And the way we think can affect how our bodies feel.

Can you imagine what it's like when you think about something really exciting?

Your whole body feels good because of your thoughts.

You might feel like you have a lot of energy, or like you want to run around and jump up and down.

Your body is doing this because of your thoughts.

But then can you imagine when you feel sick and have a really sore tummy?

Then there's a good chance that you will feel sad and fed-up.

So it's important that we learn how to have healthy thoughts and healthy bodies so we can feel good and enjoy ourselves!

Here are some things that can help you...

spend time with people you love and who love you too.

Move your body in ways that feel good!

Get plenty of time outdoors in nature and sunlight.

Play and laugh.

Eat fresh, homemade food.

Rest and relax
whenever you feel like it.

Tell someone you trust about your worries or problems.

Express all of your emotions.

Connect to the people who live in your neighbourhood.

Notice and be thankful
for what you already have.

Expect good things
to happen in your life.

Have lots of cuddles and snuggles!

Let's do these things as often as we can!

For Ana and Alex, with love.

About Dr Jane Hartley

Jane is a Holistic Health Consultant who has spent 20 years researching, teaching and writing about health.

She has pioneered research into holistic health at some of the most prestigious universities.

Jane is passionate about sharing information about holistic health in an accessible and joyful way.

drjanehartley.com

Printed in Poland
by Amazon Fulfillment
Poland Sp. z o.o., Wrocław